May your Mother's Day make you
smile and your heart blossom.

You do small things with great love.

Saint Theresa

A Nanny holds our tiny hands for just a while,
but our hearts forever.

A Nanny always has time to spare.

And a Nanny is always there.

You are the best Nanny!

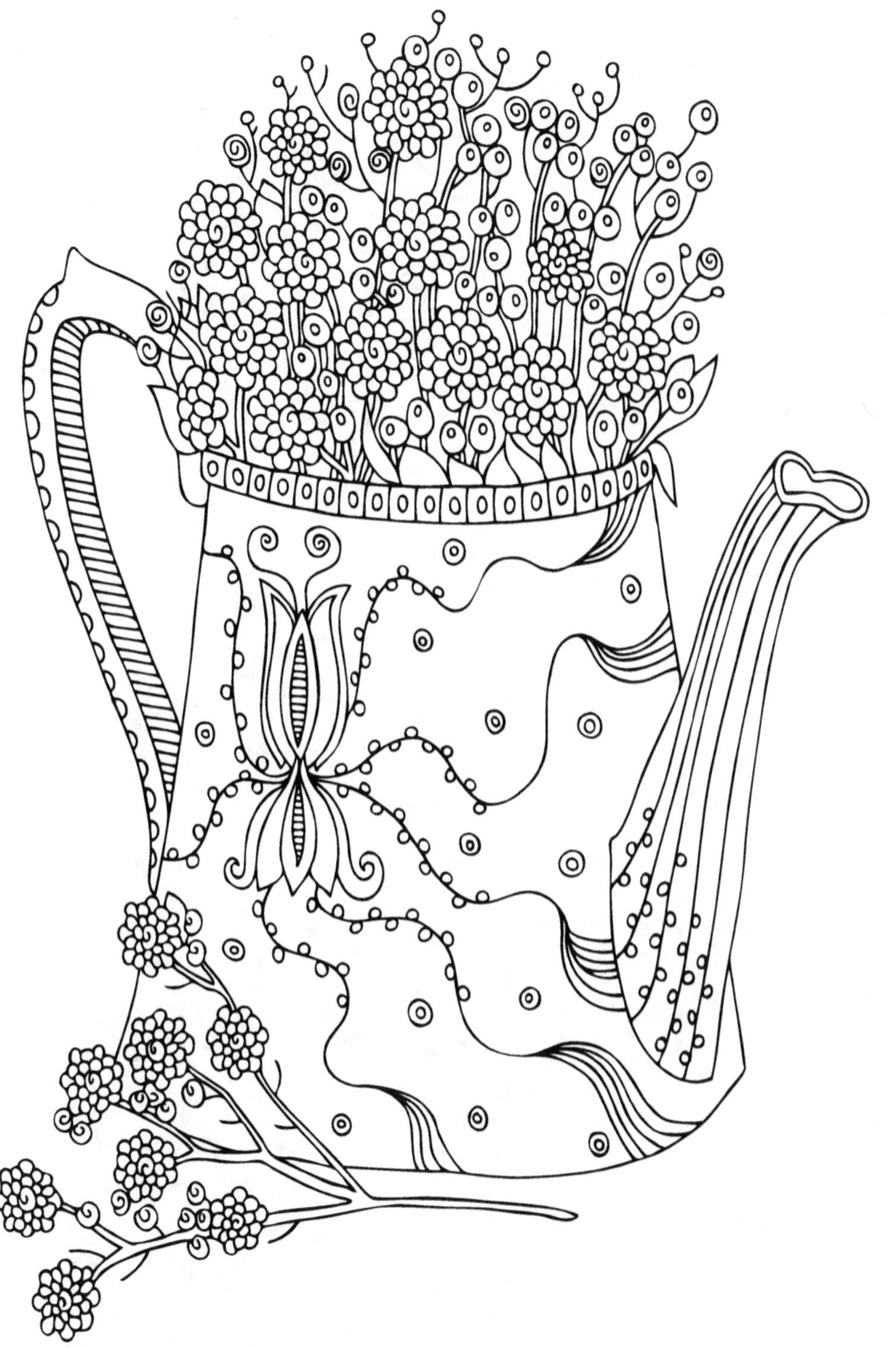

May your Mother's Day be as
bright and fun as you are!

Wishing you a day that is
just like you want it to be!

Nanny's are precious people who cause joyful happenings in the hearts of children!

Every day is special with a Nanny like you.

Every day is special with a Nanny like you.

Nanny's are moms with a bit more frosting!

Nanny's are moms with a bit more frosting!

I am so fortunate to have a Nanny like you who always takes good care of me!

You deserve to have all of your
dreams come true.

flowers for your special day!

flowers for your special day!

You are one fabulous Nanny.

Happy Mother's Day to a
Special Nanny!
(Coloring Card)
Copyright 2018

Sending warm greetings to a very special Nanny
on Mother's Day!

from,